ARTISTIC DRAWING

Kat Rakel-Ferguson

NORTH LIGHT BOOKS

cincinnati, ohio
www.artistsnetwork.com

This book is dedicated to my husband, Ray, and our kitty cats.
They draw the best out of me and paint my life with joy and love!

acknowledgements

First of all, I want to thank my editors, Maggie Moschell, Kathi Howard, and Liz Koffel. Thanks, too, to Christine Polomsky, Sally Finnegan, Greg Albert and all of the people at North Light Books.

Thanks to my sister Kim and her sons, Alex and Nick Lilly, for their love and support during this project. Additional thanks to my mother, Jean Bridges, and her husband, Jack. Their creativity inspires me.

Certainly thanks must be expressed to my teaching colleagues and friends: Mary Sue Markey, Mary Anne Donovan, Jan Harbolt, Mark Wiesner, Doris Uhlman, Gloria Brinkman, Jennifer Baldwin, Margaret Copfer, Barry Andersen, Diane Kruer and Dr. David Payne. Also, never forget Diane Hite and Mary Chieco!

07 06 05 04 03   5 4 3 2 1

Library of Congress Cataloging-in-Publication Data

Rakel-Ferguson, Kat
   Artistic drawing / by Kat Rakel-Ferguson.
      p. cm.
   Summary: Provides step-by-step instructions for a variety of drawing projects, including "Draw with Glue," "White Still Life," and "Draw Fantasy Faces."
   ISBN 1-58180-287-0 (pbk.: alk. paper)
   1. Drawing—Technique—Juvenile literature. [1. Drawing—Technique.] I. Title.

NC730 .R34 2002
741.2—dc21

2002021857

Editors: Maggie Moschell, Kathi Howard and Liz Koffel; **Cover Design:** Andrea Short; **Interior Design:** Andrea Short and Matthew DeRhodes; **Layout Artist:** Kathy Gardner; **Production Coordinator:** Kristen Heller; **Photographer:** Christine Polomsky

ABOUT THE AUTHOR

When I was about ten years old, I enrolled in a summer art class. One day, we went outside to draw trees. I drew a tree that looked like the one at the right:

When the teacher saw my drawing, she said, "Where do you see any tree that looks like that?!" Of course, there were no real trees that looked like mine. I was so embarrassed that I never returned to that art class and gave up any idea of becoming an artist even though I always felt creative.

I didn't take any art classes again until the age of twenty-nine when I took a photography course at Northern Kentucky University and discovered that I still loved art. So, I studied fine art and education and became an art teacher.

Because I will never forget the pain I felt from that first teacher's thoughtless comment, my goal as a teacher is to encourage and nurture the artistic efforts of every one of my students. Every day my students learn to express their creativity and now I hope that this book will help you discover your talent.

The author at age 10!

projects

A NOTE TO GROWN-UPS

This book was written with the curious child age 6 to 12 and busy parent in mind. Your child can successfully complete every project in this book with little or no direct adult assistance. In addition, the materials can be easily found around your house or purchased inexpensively at a grocery, discount or craft store.

Getting the Most Out of the Projects

• Although the materials listed in this book are safe, remind your child that art supplies are not food or toys.

• Designate a place for doing art projects: perhaps the kitchen table or an area in the basement or family room.

• Demonstrate for your child how to clean brushes, put away supplies and clean up the work area so your child knows how to maintain a functional art space.

• Art activities are ideal for times when your child has a friend visiting. A companion makes the activity more fun.

• If your child requests help, try to avoid working directly on his or her artwork. Draw your example on a separate piece of paper and encourage your child's efforts. The satisfaction of making something "by myself" is one of the great joys of artistic creation.

• When your budding artist brings a masterpiece for you to admire, you can begin a conversation by saying, "Tell me about your drawing," instead of, "That's nice."

• There are no mistakes in art, only discoveries. Praise your child for finding an innovative way of expressing himself or herself. After all, artistic drawing is creative drawing!

BE A GOOD ARTIST

Art and craft projects can be messy. Cover your workspace with paper or a vinyl tablecloth.

Protect your clothing with an apron or an old shirt when you are working with paint, markers or pastels.

Take care of your art supplies. Replace the caps on your markers so they don't dry out. Keep chalks in their original box so they stay as clean as possible. Stack your extra paper neatly when you are done drawing.

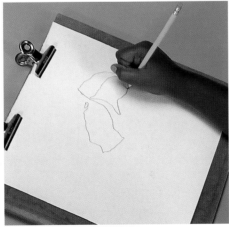

Each project has photos of the materials you'll need to make it easier for you to gather your supplies. Always clean up your workspace and put things away when you're finished.

Drawing is fun! Practice drawing every day, even if it's just for a few minutes. The more you practice, the better you'll get.

DRAWING MATERIALS

When you sit down to draw, what tools will you use?

PAPER

Try these kinds of paper for your drawings:

• **White writing paper** is good for pencils, pens and markers, but not rough enough to use with chalk and pastels.

• **Construction paper** is good for crayons, chalk, pastels and oil pastels.

• **Brown paper bags** can be used with any drawing tools.

• **Drawing paper** often comes in pads. It's rougher than writing paper and is good to use with all drawing tools.

• **Pastel or charcoal paper** is sold at art supply stores. This paper is rough and made for chalk and pastel drawings.

• **Gift wrap** comes in many exciting colors, patterns and prints. Many of the projects in this book can be made with scraps of used or leftover bits of wrapping paper.

DRAWING BOARDS

• **A drawing board**, with clips to hold your paper in place, gives you a clean, smooth surface for drawing. It is especially helpful for when you want to draw someplace without a table.

PENCILS

• **Ordinary no. 2 pencils** are fine for the projects in this book. You can buy other types of drawing pencils at craft or art supply stores if you like. Hard pencils ("H") make light marks, and softer pencils ("B") make dark marks.

• **Colored pencils** are better than crayons for coloring small areas and making thin lines. You can layer colored pencils to create new combinations.

OTHER SUPPLIES

MARKERS

• **Markers** are either washable (water-based) or permanent (these stain your clothes). The tips can be fine (thin) to broad (thick). Some markers will smear or bleed on certain kinds of paper, so it's a good idea to test your markers on the paper before you begin a project.

COLORED CHALK AND CHALK PASTELS

• **Chalks** are inexpensive and come in large buckets for sidewalk drawing or small boxes for drawing on paper. The colors are usually very pale.

• **Chalk pastels** are softer, brighter and come in many different colors. They are very easily blended. A broken edge makes a nice point for coloring tight spaces.

Pastels, chalks and oil pastels can leave your hands messy. Use wet wipes to clean your fingers so you don't get smudges on your artwork.

CRAYONS AND OIL PASTELS

• **Most crayons** are made of wax and come in dozens of colors. Crayons are inexpensive, easy to find and can be blended to make layers of colors. You can use broken crayons for coloring large areas by removing the wrapper.

• **Oil pastels** are softer than crayons. The colors are usually bright and are easily layered and blended. Artists often use oil pastels because the drawings look a lot like oil paintings.

DISPLAYING YOUR ARTWORK

Showing off your finished drawing is part of the fun. You want to make it look as good as possible. Mounting or matting your drawing will make it even more special.

Mounting

Mounting means that you simply glue your drawing onto a larger (and usually different-colored) surface. You can use cardboard or construction paper.

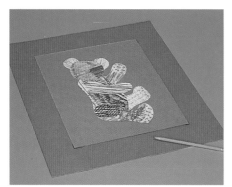

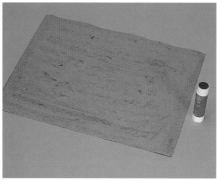

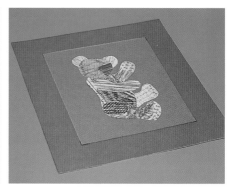

1. Use a ruler to measure the length and width of your artwork. The paper you are mounting your artwork on has to be larger than your drawing. So take your measurements and add 4" to 6" (10cm to 15cm) to them. This is how large your mounting paper has to be. Cut your mounting paper to fit these new measurements.

Center your artwork on the larger paper. Make sure it's straight. Now lightly outline the corners with a pencil.

2. Use a glue stick to cover the back of your artwork. Don't forget the edges.

3. Carefully smooth down your picture onto the larger paper, using the pencil marks as a guide.

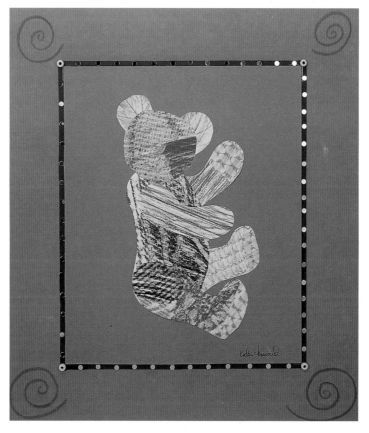

4. Decorate the mounting paper or leave it plain. Sign your name in the lower right corner of your artwork.

Matting

Matting means you cut a paper frame to go around your drawing. The opening in the mat is smaller than your artwork, so you can attach the artwork to the back of the mat with tape..

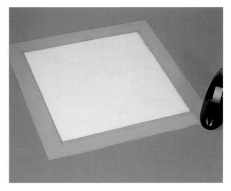

1. Cut a piece of paper or cardboard 2" to 3" (5cm to 8cm) larger than your picture. Turn it over so the front is facing down. Lay your drawing on top of your matting paper. Center it and lightly outline its shape.

2. Draw a rectangle inside the first one about ¼" (6mm) smaller on all four sides, and then cut it out.

3. Place your artwork face down over the opening and tape it in place.

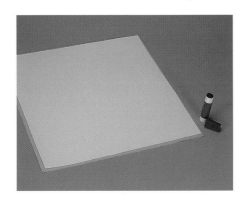

4. To make the mat stronger, cut another piece of cardboard the same size as the mat and glue it on the back of the matted picture.

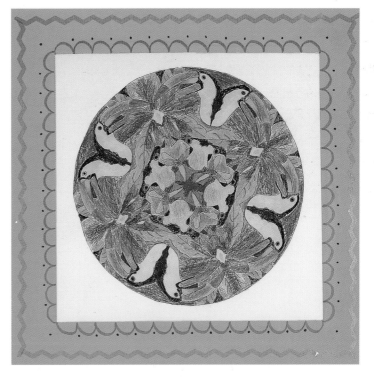

5. You can leave the mat plain or decorate it with stamps, glitter, buttons or drawings. Don't forget to sign your name in the lower right corner of your artwork.

No Peeking

TO DRAW REALISTICALLY, you have to look at objects closely. Find shapes that make up the object you are drawing. As your eyes slowly follow the object's edges, your hand will draw lines the same way. These lines are called contours. We call this art **CONTOUR DRAWING**. Can you do an entire drawing without peeking at the paper? Don't worry if your drawings look funny. You'll improve with practice!

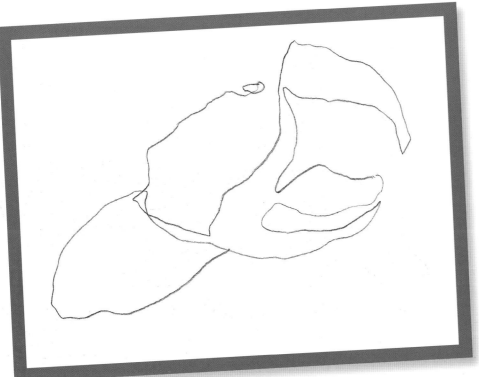

● **THIS BASEBALL CAP** looks pretty good for not peeking. See if you can recognize all the objects you try to draw without looking at the paper.

SUPPLIES

pencil

drawing board
with clips and paper

large paper

DON'T PEEK! Since you aren't looking at your paper, your lines will be the right shapes, just not in the right places, like in this drawing of a teapot.

NOW PEEK After you've practiced not looking at your drawing, you can start glancing at the paper while you draw, but most of the time you should still be looking closely at the object.

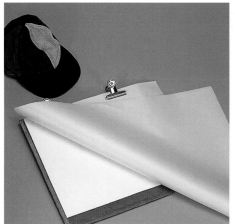

1. Choose an object to draw. Cover your drawing paper with a larger piece of paper so you can't see what you're drawing. Put your hand under this top sheet while you draw. Remember, don't look at your paper!

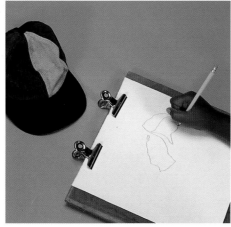

2. Pretend there is a string connecting your eye and the pencil. Slowly move your eye and your pencil at the same time. Keep your pencil on the paper all the time and no peeking!

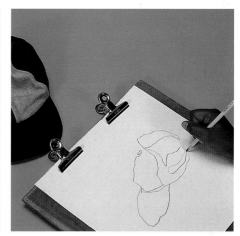

3. When the drawing is finished, you can look! It's OK if your drawing isn't perfect. Drawing without peeking is just learning to see and draw the length, shape and direction of each line. This is your first step to drawing realistically.

Draw With Glue

Y OU DON'T ALWAYS NEED A PENCIL TO DRAW! Using glue adds a fun

and interesting dimension to your pictures. Try this project and then

draw anything you want using glue for your lines. Let the glue dry until

it's clear before adding color. If you're in a hurry, dry it with a hair dryer.

• SEE HOW THIS LEAF is outlined with the glue? It adds interesting texture to your drawing. You can draw anything with glue. See how many objects you can find and draw with glue.

SUPPLIES

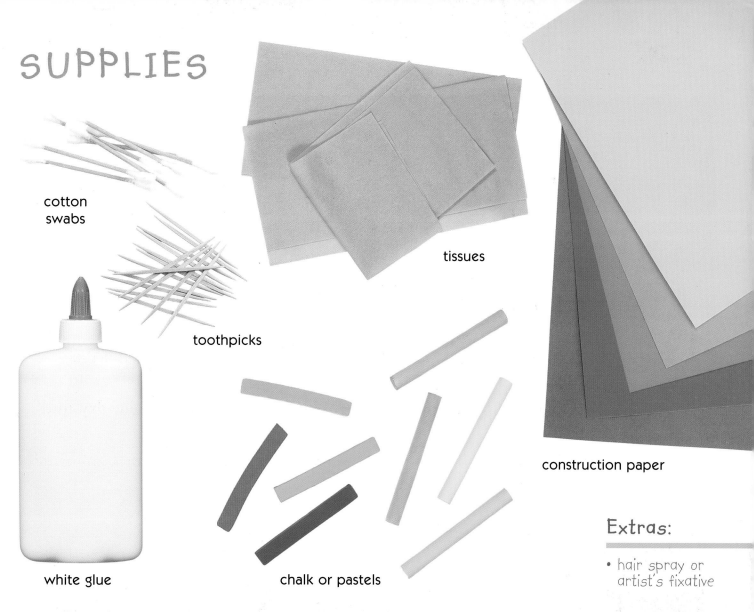

cotton swabs

tissues

toothpicks

white glue

chalk or pastels

construction paper

Extras:
• hair spray or artist's fixative

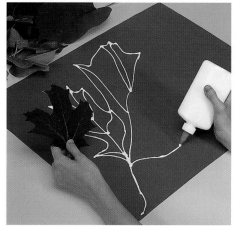

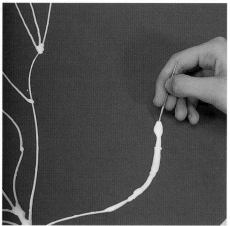

1. Choose an interesting subject to draw. Now look and find the shapes that make up that object. Use white glue to draw the outlines of these shapes onto a colored piece of paper.

2. If the glue puddles instead of making a line, drag a toothpick through the puddle. Let the glue dry completely before going on to the next step.

3. When the glue is clear, use chalk or pastels to color the spaces between the lines. Be creative and use any colors you want. This is your drawing. You don't have to use the colors everyone expects your subject to be!

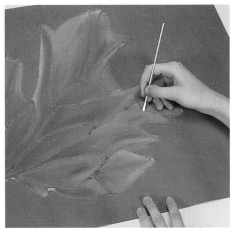

4. Use your fingers or a tissue to blend light and dark colors to make your picture more exciting. Shake extra chalk dust into the trash—don't blow it away!

5. Continue to add more colors and blend them until your drawing is finished.

6. Carefully clean the chalk off the glue lines with a tissue or cotton swab. Ask an adult to lightly spray your picture with hair spray or artist's fixative so the chalk doesn't rub off.

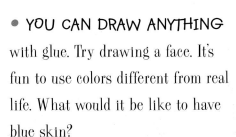

MORE IDEAS!

● **YOU CAN DRAW ANYTHING** with glue. Try drawing a face. It's fun to use colors different from real life. What would it be like to have blue skin?

● **THE DELICATE COLORS** in this dragonfly come from making this drawing on typing paper, which is smooth and doesn't hold chalk well. If you like bright colors, use rougher paper. If you want pale colors, use smoother paper.

● **DRAWING SMALL** or thin places, such as these car tires, is easier when you use a cotton swab to blend the pastels. Use a toothpick to spread thin lines of glue.

Draw Your World

Drawing the world you see can be pretty tricky. This project will help you learn how to make spaces and objects look real on a flat surface. This is called **PERSPECTIVE DRAWING**. When we draw things using perspective we are looking at how big or small objects appear when we compare them to other objects.

● **SIZES CAN SURPRISE YOU!** You know a car is larger than a small bush. But when the car is far away and the bush is up close, as in the picture above, you have to draw the car much smaller than the bush. That's perspective!

● **SEEING THINGS IN PERSPECTIVE** is easy when you trace what you see. All you need is a window, a sheet of acetate and some permanent markers.

SUPPLIES

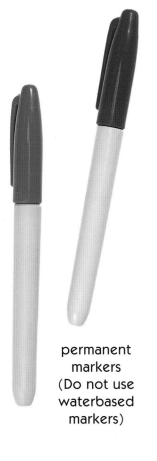

permanent
markers
(Do not use
waterbased
markers)

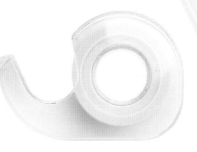

clear tape

clear plastic
report cover or
piece of acetate

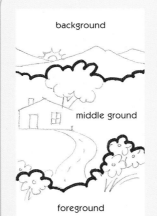

background

middle ground

foreground

BACKGROUND is the stuff farthest away. It usually looks the smallest (even if it's really big), and should appear in the upper part of your picture.

MIDDLE GROUND is the stuff in the middle.

FOREGROUND is the stuff closest to you and should appear larger and lower on your picture.

1. Cut a clear report cover on the fold (or use a sheet of acetate) and tape it to a window. Look for a window with a view that has a interesting foreground, background and middle ground.

2. Use a permanent marker to trace what you see. If you move your head, the view will change, so keep your head still.

3. Once you finish tracing your subject, remove the drawing from the window, add color and you're done!

Draw Real Stuff!

DRAWING FROM YOUR IMAGINATION is fun, but how do you learn to draw something that looks like what you really see? Here are some fun exercises to do that will help you draw things that look real!

● **LOOK AT THIS WHITE BALL.**

It isn't white, is it? It's different shades of gray. A drawing of a circle can be made to look like a real ball just by shading it gradually from dark to light.

● **THIS BALL WAS DRAWN** on colored paper with pastels. Since the paper is not white, the artist used white chalk to color in the lightest part of the ball.

SUPPLIES

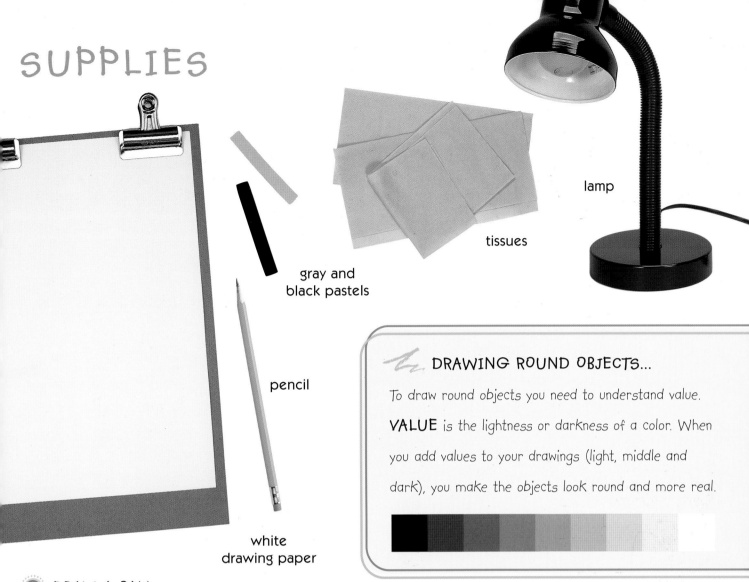

lamp

tissues

gray and
black pastels

pencil

white
drawing paper

✎ DRAWING ROUND OBJECTS...

To draw round objects you need to understand value.

VALUE is the lightness or darkness of a color. When you add values to your drawings (light, middle and dark), you make the objects look round and more real.

 DRAW A BALL

1. Place a white ball in front of you and shine a light on it from the right side. Trace a circle on your paper to begin. Look at the shadow the ball casts. Use a black pastel or pencil to add a shadow on the paper to the left of the ball.

2. Now look at the shadows on the ball. Shade the darkest side of the ball opposite the light. Use a tissue to blend some of the pencil so it is darkest on the edge of the ball and becomes lighter towards the center of the ball.

3. The lightest value of your ball is white. Lightly shade the background to make the white part of the ball stand out. Your circle should now look like a real ball.

21

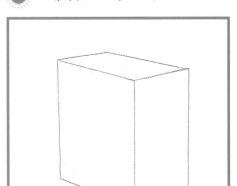
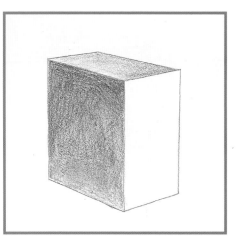

1. Look closely at the box in the photo below. There are light, medium and dark values with a straight line between each value. Each surface has its own value. Start with a pencil sketch of the box. Use a ruler to draw straight lines.

2. Fill in and blend the darkest value on the left side of the box with a black pastel or a dark pencil. Fill in the top of the box with a medium shade of gray, either with a pencil, a gray pastel or by coloring in and lightly blending a black pastel.

3. Add a dark shadow to the left side of the box so that it looks like it is resting on the ground. This should be the darkest part of your drawing. Lightly shade in the background so that the white side of the box pops out.

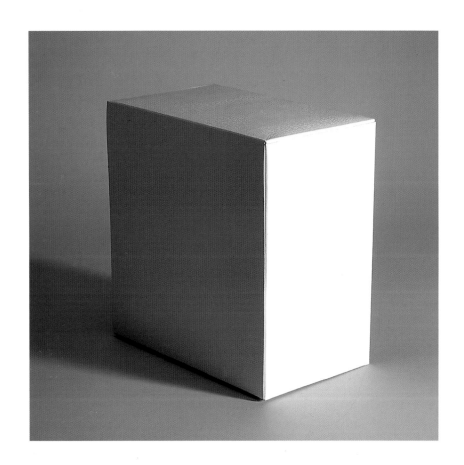

● **LOOK CLOSELY** at the box. Each side of the box is a different value—light, medium or dark. Unlike the ball, these changes are not gradual; they are very distinct. Other box-like objects can be drawn the same way: a house, your TV, or even a skyscraper! Just look for the values.

● ADDING PERSPECTIVE

This photo shows a pitcher. What shape is the opening in the top of the pitcher? How would you draw this opening? Try to draw the pitcher using the shapes that you see.

WRONG PERSPECTIVE. This drawing doesn't look right because the oval opening is drawn too round, like a circle. Look at the photo of the pitcher again. See how the opening is really shaped. It's not round, is it?

RIGHT PERSPECTIVE. This drawing is better; it looks like the original pitcher. The oval shape of the opening at the top and the curve of the bottom of the pitcher are more accurate.

◎ WATCH FOR CHANGING SHAPES!

You may think that the front of a building looks like a rectangle but, depending on where you stand, the shape can actually change! If you look straight down over a dinner plate, it looks like a circle. Look at it again from the side and its shape seems to change into an oval. This exercise will help you draw the shapes you see.

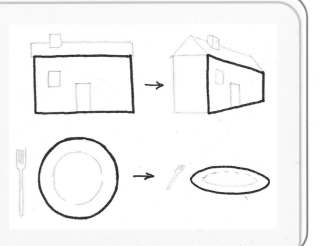

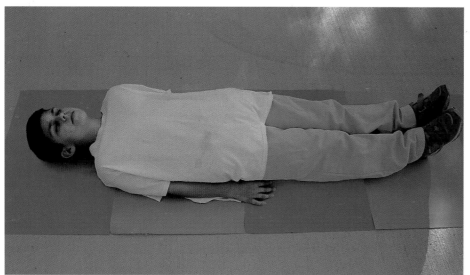

● USE THIS TECHNIQUE for another way to make your drawings look realistic. Foreshortening is when you draw something shorter than it really is. One part of an object may look like it is larger because it is closer to you than another part of the object. It is a lot like drawing perspective.

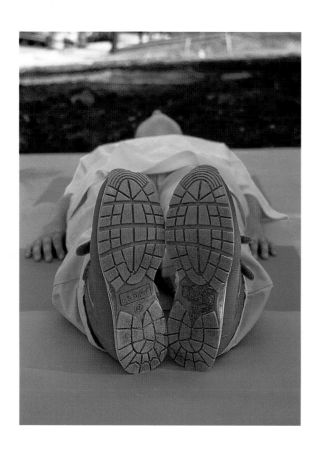

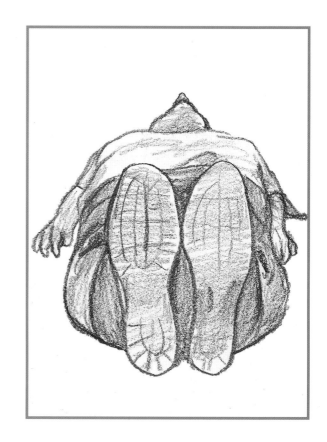

● LOOK AT THIS BOY FROM HIS FEET. His feet look huge and his head looks tiny. His feet aren't really larger than his head, but you would draw them that way because that's how they look. Now draw this boy!

THE COLORED PIECES OF PAPER in the photo on the upper left are all the same size when seen from above. The boy's head and feet look normal. The boy is not foreshortened. Notice below when the boy is pictured from his head or feet, things that are closer to the front are larger then the things in the back. Now the boy is foreshortened. Look at the colored squares. Do you see how they change size, too?

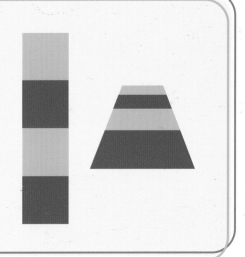

● LOOK AT THE SAME BOY from the opposite end. His head looks big and his feet look very small. You draw his head larger than his feet because that's how it looks. Try drawing the boy now!

White Still Life

A STILL LIFE IS A COLLECTION OF OBJECTS that an artist sets up to draw or paint. When you draw a still life, you'll get to practice the drawing skills you learned in Draw Real Stuff (page 20). You will be using different values to draw round, square and oval objects correctly. You will also use foreshortening when something is coming toward you. Working with white objects will help you see the highlights and shadows caused by light.

● **WHY WHITE?** It's easier to learn to draw white objects because all you have to do is match the black, white and gray values. You can draw on colored paper, but try to keep your still life all white so you don't have to worry about values and colors all at the same time.

SUPPLIES

gray paper

paper towels

cotton swabs

pencil

35mm slide mount (remove the slide)

white and black pastels or chalk

lamp or flashlight

Extras:
- hair spray or artist's fixative

1. Arrange some white objects on a table in a darkened room. Shine a bright lamp or flashlight from the side of your still life so you can easily see the shadows (darks) and highlights (lights).

2. Look through your viewfinder to select the part of your still life that you want to draw. (Turn to page 28 to learn how to make and use a viewfinder.)

3. Use a pencil to draw the contours of your still life on your gray paper.

4. Use the black pastel or chalk to color in the dark areas of your still life. Remember to look closely and find different values of darks. Use a cotton swab to blend the darks so that you create different values within your drawing.

5. Use white chalk or pastel to add the highlights or light areas to your drawing. Make sure you blend the lights with the darks to create different values. But don't blend too much or it will become one gray drawing!

HERE ARE JUST A FEW WHITE OBJECTS YOU MAY WANT TO DRAW:

- white flowers
- white shoes
- white soccer ball
- white plates or dishes
- white cardboard boxes
- white plastic bottles
- white books

KIDS! Try this!

MAKE YOUR OWN VIEWFINDER...

A viewfinder is a great tool to help you *see* better. Ask your parent for an old slide and cut the image out of the frame or cut a window out of white cardboard. Use your viewfinder to frame part of the scene you are looking at—like a camera that focuses only on what you are taking a picture of.

- Turn your paper the same way as your viewfinder, either horizontally or vertically.
- Draw only what you *see* in the window of your viewfinder. If an object is cut off, that's OK. Don't draw the part you can't *see*.

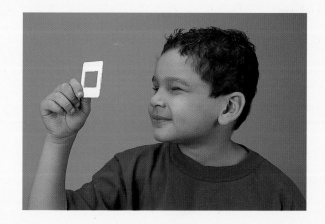

 FOR VARIETY AND MORE FUN, use colored paper and colored chalks instead of black and white. Just make sure you pay close attention to the values you are drawing. Remember, if you want something to look real, you need to draw the values correctly. Find the highlights and the shadows and you'll do great!

(tip)

• Don't blend too much or your drawing will become one shade of gray. If this happens, add dark chalk to the very darkest parts and light chalk to the very lightest parts.

• When you're finished, ask an adult to spray your picture lightly with hair spray or artist's fixative to keep it from smearing.

29

Draw With Stencils

DRAWING WITH STENCILS IS A GREAT WAY to play with shapes. Cover parts of your drawing paper with stencils cut from construction paper and rub chalk over them. It leaves the shape of your stencil on the paper. You can use stencils to draw any type of landscape or scene.

● WHEN CREATING A LANDSCAPE remember to include a foreground, middle ground and background.

SUPPLIES

construction paper

Extras:

Extras:

• hair spray or artist's fixative

pencil

colored chalk or pastels

DON'T FORGET...

Pastels and chalk can be very messy! Use moist baby wipes to keep your fingers clean. Try to keep fingerprints off your drawings. Neatness counts!

paper towels or tissues

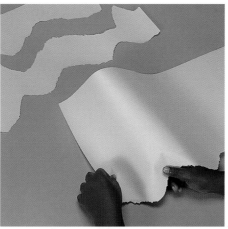

1. Sketch a landscape scene. Include objects in the background, middle ground and foreground. Use this drawing as your guide.

2. Use a separate piece of paper to tear or cut out shapes that are similar to your background shapes. This torn paper will be the hills in the background.

3. Carefully coat the edges of these shapes by coloring them with chalk or pastels. These mountains were coated with blue to make the sky.

31

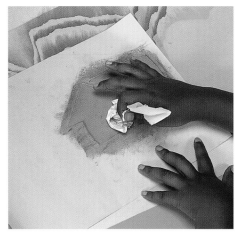

4. Lay the chalk-coated piece of paper on your drawing paper. Use a tissue or paper towel to rub the chalk carefully onto your drawing paper.

5. Keep adding chalk to the torn background shapes and rub off the colors. Leave a little space between background shapes. You can use shapes more than once with different colors.

6. To make a solid object like this house, cut the shape out of paper. Add color around the edges of the shape and then rub the color inside to fill it in.

Get creative!! Stencil drawings are easy to make and they're lots of fun too!

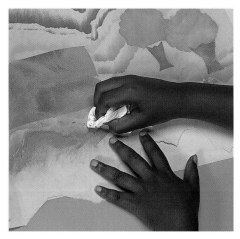

7. Add details with chalk and soften the marks with a tissue. Cut out smaller shapes to make other details.

8. Continue tearing and cutting shapes to finish the middle ground of your picture.

9. Create more shapes and color edges to make your foreground. It's OK for shapes to overlap each other. To keep the chalk from smearing, ask an adult to spray your drawing with hair spray or artist's fixative.

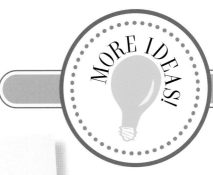

● THESE TROPICAL
FISH were drawn two
different ways. The red
fish was made by coloring
inside a fish-shaped stencil. The orange fish was
made by coloring around
the outside edges of paper
cut in the shape of a fish.

● RACE CARS SPEED BY in
this stencil drawing. The faces in
the background are small and look
like dots. The cars in the foreground
are overlapped to make them look
as if they were passing each other.

Sun Catchers

Y OU CAN MAKE YOUR OWN PAPER and add your drawing to it to create your own sun catchers. For this bright idea you'll be using tissue paper, glue and your own creativity. If you tape your drawings to a sunny window, they will fill the room with color!

● THIS BRIGHT TROPICAL FISH will look great hanging in a sunny window. Other colorful subjects such as a rainbow, a bird or a race car also make good sun catchers.

SUPPLIES

scissors

black marker

colored tissue paper

white glue

report cover or piece of acetate

paintbrush

1. Gather several sheets of different colored tissue paper. Tear the paper into different-sized pieces. Tear off the sharp edges of the paper so that the pieces blend together better.

2. Pour white glue into a dish. Dip your brush in water, then into the glue. Paint the watery glue on a clear plastic report cover. Place torn tissue paper pieces on the glue. Overlap your pieces and paint watery glue on any dry paper.

3. Place three or four layers of tissue paper and glue. Let each layer dry before adding another.

35

4. When you've covered the report cover with three or four layers of tissue paper and they are completely dry, slowly peel your newly created sheet of paper from the plastic.

5. Use a dark-colored marker to draw on your handmade paper. Using a black marker makes your drawing look like a stained-glass window.

6. Cut out your drawing and hang it in a window.

MORE IDEAS!

● **BRIGHT YELLOW RAYS** of sunshine make this a perfect sun catcher for any window. How about a drawing of the moon and planets? The four seasons?

● THIS FISH WINDSOCK was made by wrapping homemade paper around a 2-liter plastic bottle and taping the seam. The scales and eyes were drawn, then the tail was added. Holes were punched at the top for the string.

● DRAWINGS IN SOFT COLORS can be used for making sun catchers, too. When you make your handmade paper, use white paper napkins or white tissue paper instead of brightly colored tissue paper. It's fun to draw on this paper with colored pencils.

37

Draw Yourself

Drawing portraits is much easier than you might think. In fact, drawing a portrait is like following a map. Follow these simple directions and you will be drawing portraits of yourself and your friends before you know it!

● TO MAKE A PORTRAIT LOOK REAL, you have to put every part of your face in the right place. See how the corners of the nose line up with the inside corners of the eyes, and the corners of the mouth are below the centers of the eyes? Look at the diagram on page 40 to learn more about how to correctly draw your face.

SUPPLIES

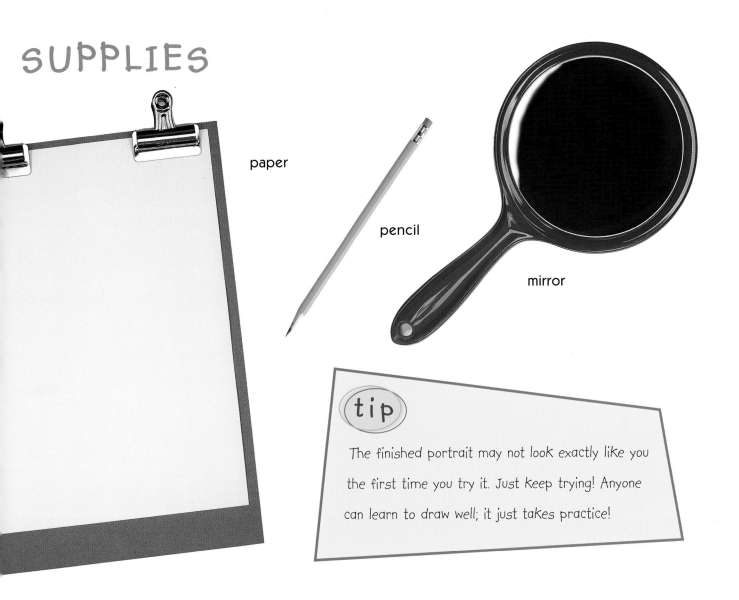

paper

pencil

mirror

tip

The finished portrait may not look exactly like you the first time you try it. Just keep trying! Anyone can learn to draw well; it just takes practice!

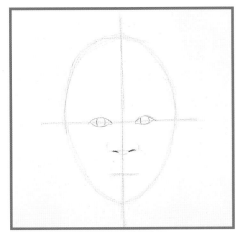

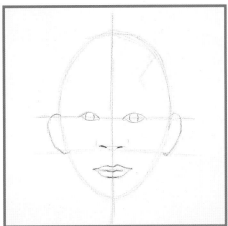

1. Sit in front of a mirror and draw a large oval. This is your face. With a pencil, divide the oval in half from ear to ear and from hair to chin. Now refer to the diagram on page 40 and draw the eyes, nose and mouth where they belong.

2. Draw your lips halfway between your nose and chin Add your ears. The tops of your ears line up with your eyes. The bottoms of your ears will be at the same level as the tip of your nose.

3. Draw your hair using a few lines and some shading. Add your eyebrows above your eyes. Add some shading to your ears so you can give them some depth.

4. Look at your neck in the mirror. Now, draw your neck and shoulders. Make sure you draw your neck wide enough.

5. Use the side of your pencil to make shadows for the sides of the nose. Draw other details such as your favorite jewelry, ball cap or patterns on your clothes.

6. Add shadows on your neck, lips and clothing.

KIDS! Check this out!

This drawing shows how the parts of the human face line up. The eyes are in the middle, halfway between the top of the head and the chin. The tops of the ears line up with the eyes. The nose is a third to halfway between the eyes and chin.

MATCHING THE TWO SIDES OF YOUR FACE...

To make the two halves of the face match, lightly draw a vertical line down the center of the face. This helps you compare the two halves of your drawing and adjust anything that doesn't match.

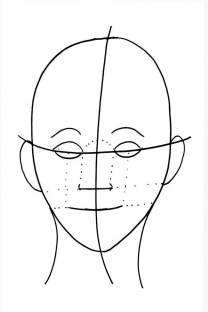

● **THIS BOY WITH GLASSES** is smiling. What emotions can you show in your portrait?

● **THIS GIRL WITH LONG HAIR** added birds and trees to the background of her self-portrait.

Fantasy Faces

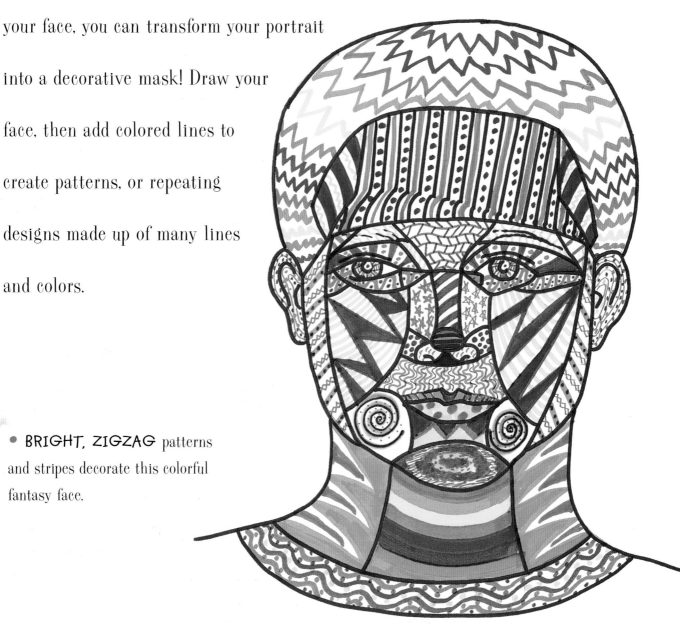

NOW THAT YOU KNOW HOW TO DRAW

your face, you can transform your portrait

into a decorative mask! Draw your

face, then add colored lines to

create patterns, or repeating

designs made up of many lines

and colors.

● **BRIGHT, ZIGZAG** patterns
and stripes decorate this colorful
fantasy face.

SUPPLIES

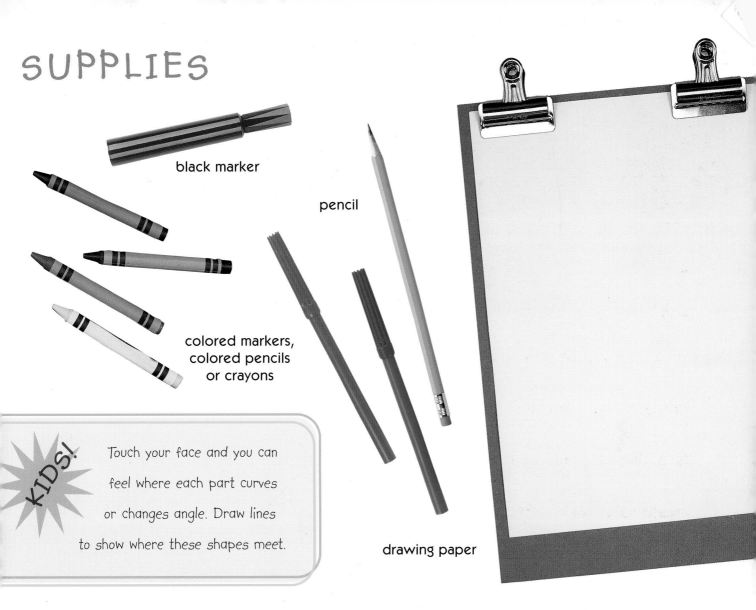

black marker

pencil

colored markers,
colored pencils
or crayons

drawing paper

KIDS! Touch your face and you can feel where each part curves or changes angle. Draw lines to show where these shapes meet.

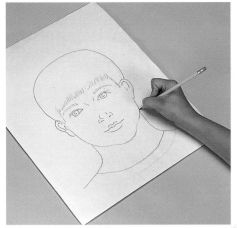

1. Start with a pencil sketch of your face. (See Draw Yourself, page 38.)

2. Look for the different shapes that make up your face. Use these shapes to divide your face into large sections. Keep the drawing balanced—if you have a shape on the left side of the face, draw the same shape on the right side.

3. Now find even smaller shapes and keep dividing your drawing into sections until you have created a balanced drawing.

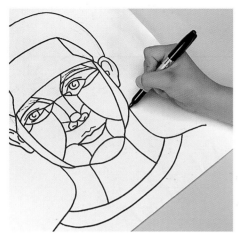

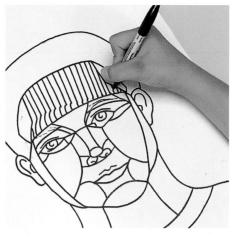

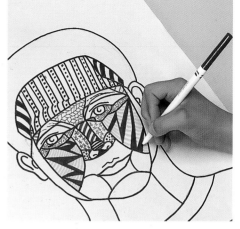

4. Take a black permanent or water-based marker and outline your drawing.

5. Use the marker to begin creating your pattern.

6. Use colored markers, pencils or crayons to add details that make patterns on your fantasy face. Be creative and use as many colors as you want. Create a new face for you to show the world.

MORE IDEAS!

• **CURVY STRIPES** on this face make the girl look happy. Think about what emotions you can show in the patterns on your fantasy face.

● **IN THIS FACE** the hair looks like curling waves and the cheeks look like sunbursts. What patterns do you see in the shapes on your face?

● **THE MOON, STARS** and the sea make beautiful patterns on this fantasy face.

45

Stuff Yourself

Did you ever want to have a twin of yourself? Now is your chance! You'll make a life-sized stuffed imitation of yourself, using paper bags and newspaper. Use your creativity as you decorate your stuffed self-portrait. Color yourself wearing a favorite shirt or shoes.

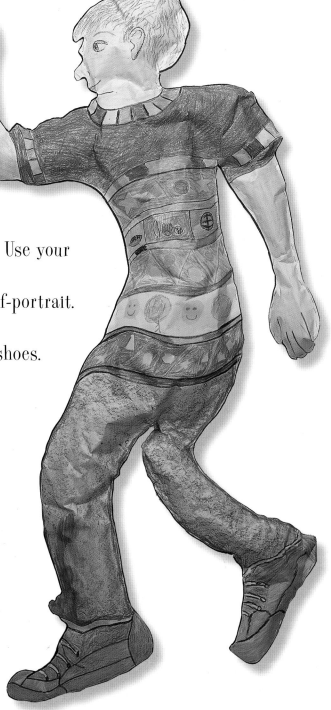

HEY KIDS! **Try this!**

YOU CAN CHOOSE any pose you want for your stuffed person. This portrait of a boy looks as if it is running.

SUPPLIES

tape

pencil

paint, crayons
or markers

black
marker

stapler

newspaper
for stuffing

paper bags
(or large sheet of paper)

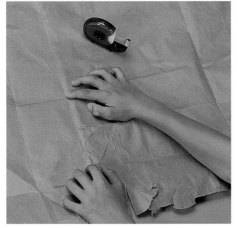

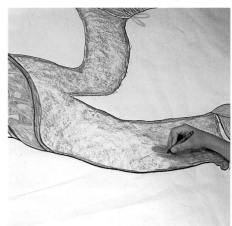

1. If you don't have paper as big as you are, tape grocery bags together until you have enough paper to trace your whole body. Remember you need two layers—one for a front and one for a back—so do this two times!

2. Lay the two large pieces of paper on the floor, one on top of the other—these will be the front and back. Ask a parent or friend to use a marker to trace around your body on the top sheet of paper.

3. Now use paint, crayons or markers to add clothes, shoes, hair and features on the front piece of paper.

47

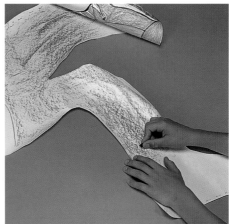

4. Cut out the drawing. Be sure that you cut through both sheets of paper. If you have trouble cutting two sheets of paper at once, cut the top sheet with your drawing on it first. Then lay your cutout figure on the bottom sheet of paper and trace the cutout using a pencil. Then cut out the second sheet.

5. Turn the second cutout sheet over and draw your back. What do you look like from behind? Use a mirror to help you see your backside if you need to. What does your head look like? What is on the back of your shoes? Use the same colors you used on the front.

6. Staple or tape the front and back together, stuffing crumpled newspaper scraps inside as you staple or tape. Be careful, the paper tears easily and staples can be sharp, so don't cut yourself. It's a good idea to put tape underneath any areas that start to tear.

 DRAWING PEOPLE...

Like the face, the human body has certain proportions.

• People are about 7 1/2 heads tall.

• When your arms hang at your sides, your fingertips will touch the middle of your thighs.

• Each hand is the same size as your face.

• Elbows are halfway from your shoulders to your wrists.

• Your knees are halfway from your heels to your hips.

• Did you know your foot is the same size as your forearm? Measure it and see!

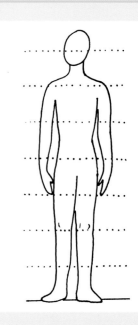

● **TEMPERA PAINT** can also be used instead of crayons or markers to color your portrait.

● **YOU CAN RECYCLE** any strong paper to make a stuffed figure. This portrait was drawn on paper bags that were taped together and then painted.

Draw With Textures

THE BEST THING ABOUT MAKING RUBBINGS is looking for unusual TEXTURES, such as the great pattern that's probably on the bottom of your shoe. Texture is the roughness or smoothness of an object or surface.

You can capture lots of textures by placing paper oven an object and rubbing its texture onto the paper with a wrapperless crayon.

● TRANSFORM YOUR TEXTURES into fun collage drawings. A collage (pronounced "koh-lah-j") is made of papers that are cut out and pasted together to form a picture.

SUPPLIES

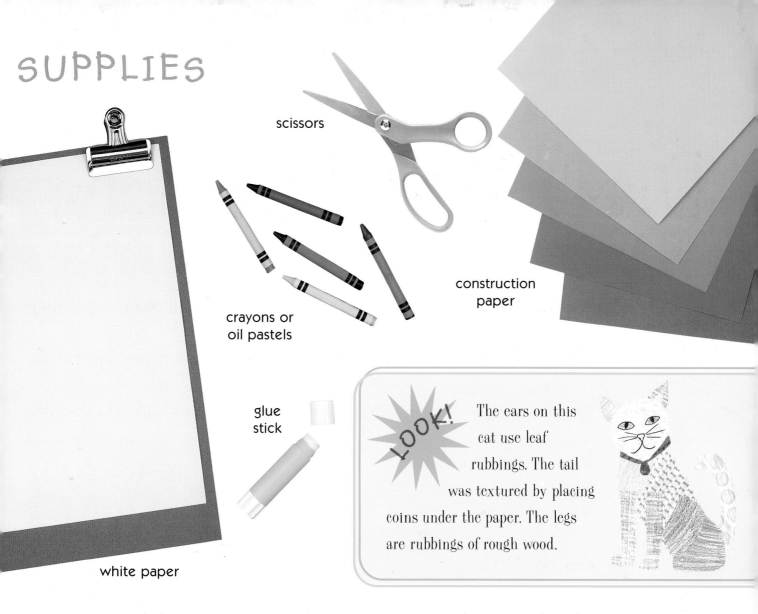

scissors

crayons or
oil pastels

construction
paper

glue
stick

white paper

LOOK! The ears on this cat use leaf rubbings. The tail was textured by placing coins under the paper. The legs are rubbings of rough wood.

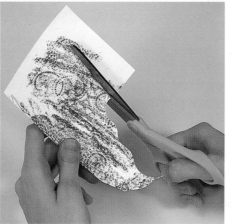

1. Find surfaces with interesting textures: your shoe tread, tree bark, a sidewalk—anything with a rough surface. Lay a piece of paper on the surface and rub the flat edge of an unwrapped crayon over it. The texture will appear on your paper.

2. Draw a picture on the textured papers and cut out the shapes. The picture on the right is made of clouds, grass and a fancy bird. You could make a face with the texture of a brick, or a fish that has the pattern from a gym shoe.

3. Glue your cut out shapes onto a piece of construction paper to make a colorful scene. You can make greeting cards, book covers and more with these pictures. Your possibilities are endless!

Draw Creatively

ARTISTS OFTEN "PLAY" with their subjects by making a series of

drawings in different and imaginative ways. This is a great project to do

on those days when you don't know what to do. Your creative juices will

be flowing in no time!

● **ABSTRACTION IS FUN!** It's a game where you look at an object and think, "how can I make that different and look totally new?" Mix up shapes and colors. Change lines and values. Be creative and see what you can make.

SUPPLIES

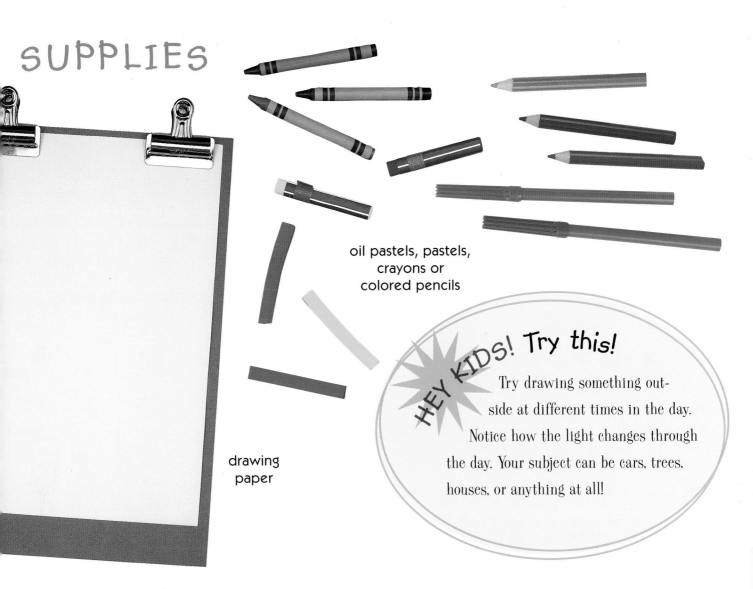

oil pastels, pastels,
crayons or
colored pencils

drawing
paper

HEY KIDS! Try this!

Try drawing something outside at different times in the day.
Notice how the light changes through
the day. Your subject can be cars, trees,
houses, or anything at all!

1. Choose a subject for your drawing. You can either draw something in your house or use a favorite photo or a picture taken from a book or magazine.

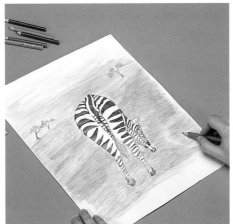

2. Create a realistic drawing. Make your drawing look as true-to-life as possible. This zebra was drawn with colored pencil, but you can use crayons, markers, colored pencils or pastels.

3. Create an abstract drawing. Look at your first drawing and decide what you want to change about your subject. Find the basic shapes and lines and focus on those. Change the colors, shapes or sizes or draw whatever you can imagine.

53

● **THE SAME CAT WAS USED** for both of these drawings. Can you believe that? The drawing above is a realistic drawing, made using the actual shapes, colors and values that you would see if you looked at that cat.

The drawing on the right is an abstraction. This is the artist's idea of the cat. She changed the color and the shapes to show how she felt about the cat, not just what she saw. Can you draw an abstract cat?

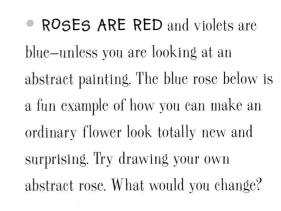

● **ROSES ARE RED** and violets are blue—unless you are looking at an abstract painting. The blue rose below is a fun example of how you can make an ordinary flower look totally new and surprising. Try drawing your own abstract rose. What would you change?

What's In Your Head?

WHAT DO YOU DREAM ABOUT? What do you want to be when you grow up? Where would you go if you could go anywhere? Everyone has hopes and dreams. Drawing what's in your head helps you to record those dreams. Plus it's a fun way to picture how all those hopes and dreams are stored in you brain.

● DREAMS, FEARS AND FAVORITE HOBBIES fill the pictures in this head. What do you think about every day?

SUPPLIES

scissors

glue
stick

colored
pencils,
markers or
crayons

colored
construction
paper

white
drawing
paper

pencil

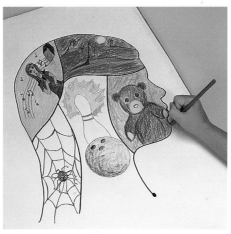

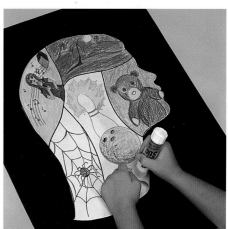

1. Draw a large side view of your head. Divide your head shape into three, five or more sections. The shapes of these sections can be large or small, divided by straight or wavy lines.

2. Draw a different picture in each area that tells something about you. Draw what you want for your future, your favorite place to visit, or your family. This can be any dream, memory or idea you have about yourself.

3. If you wish, you can add glitter, buttons or anything that you think would be fun. When you are finished, cut out the silhouette and glue it onto a piece of colored paper.

Kaleidoscopes

HAVE YOU EVER LOOKED THROUGH A KALEIDOSCOPE? Mirrors inside a tube create patterns by reflecting the beads inside it or the view of the world you see through the tube. The secret to these dazzling patterns is that the mirrors reflect the same design again and again. You can make a drawing that looks just like a kaleido-scope by tracing and flip-ping a pattern that you draw yourself. It's easy!

● **CAN YOU FIND** the initials hiding in this drawing? Bright markers made this kaleidoscope drawing look like a stained glass window.

SUPPLIES

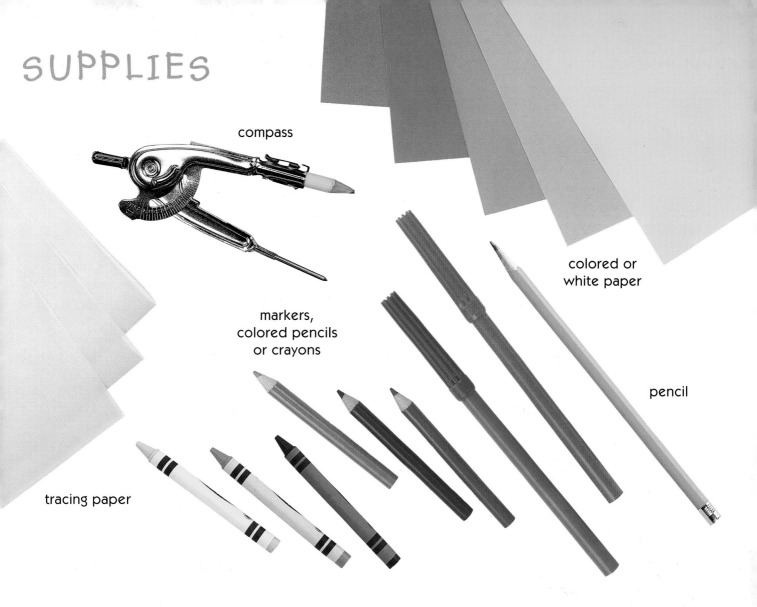

compass

colored or
white paper

markers,
colored pencils
or crayons

pencil

tracing paper

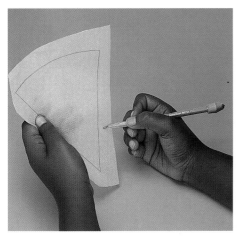 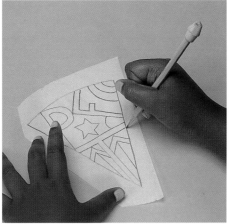 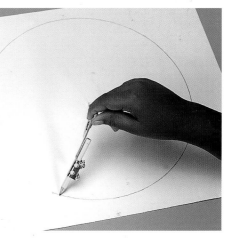

1. Trace one of the pie shapes from page 62 onto a sheet of tracing paper. This project uses the large yellow pie shape on page 62.

2. Use a pencil to draw a design in this pie shape by tracing over a photograph or making up your own design. We used the initials PTF and placed them creatively within the pie shape.

3. Choose a piece of paper large enough for your final design. Look on page 62 for the final sizes listed with the pie shapes. Use a compass to make a circle the size mentioned on your pie shape.

4. Flip your tracing paper over and place it in the circle. Make sure it lines up with the outer circle. Carefully trace over all your pencil lines. Trace the straight edges of the pie shape too. This will transfer your original pencil drawing onto the paper.

5. In the large circle, use a marker to trace over your pencil lines, except for the edges of the pie shape. Erase the pencil lines. Next, flip the tracing paper over again and place it beside the first pie wedge. Trace over all your pencil lines once more to transfer the drawing again.

6. Repeat Steps 4 and 5 until the entire circle is filled. If your pattern has a mirror, or opposite, image, you will have to use the other side of your tracing paper to make a reversed image. Then use markers, colored pencils or crayons to color your kaleidoscope picture.

● **DOTS AND STRIPES** turn into a brilliant burst of colorful patterns in this picture. This image uses the six-part pattern on page 62.

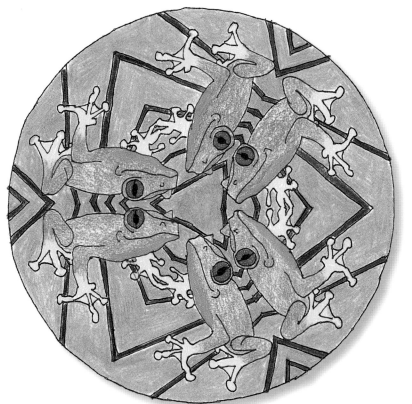

● **THIS SIX-PART DESIGN** was colored with colored pencils. It was traced from a photo of a tree frog. Use the six-part pattern on page 62 to make this design.

● **THIS DESIGN WAS MADE** from a drawing using the initials AJS. Use the four-part pattern on page 62 to create this design or you can make your own.

PATTERNS

You'll trace this shape
six times in a 9" (23cm) circle.

You'll trace this pie shape
eight times in a 12" (30cm) circle.

You'll trace this pie shape four
times in a 9" (23cm) circle.

• **USE THESE PATTERNS** to
create different-sized kaleidoscopes.
Look at the sizes listed with each
pie shape so that you will know how
large each finished circle will be.

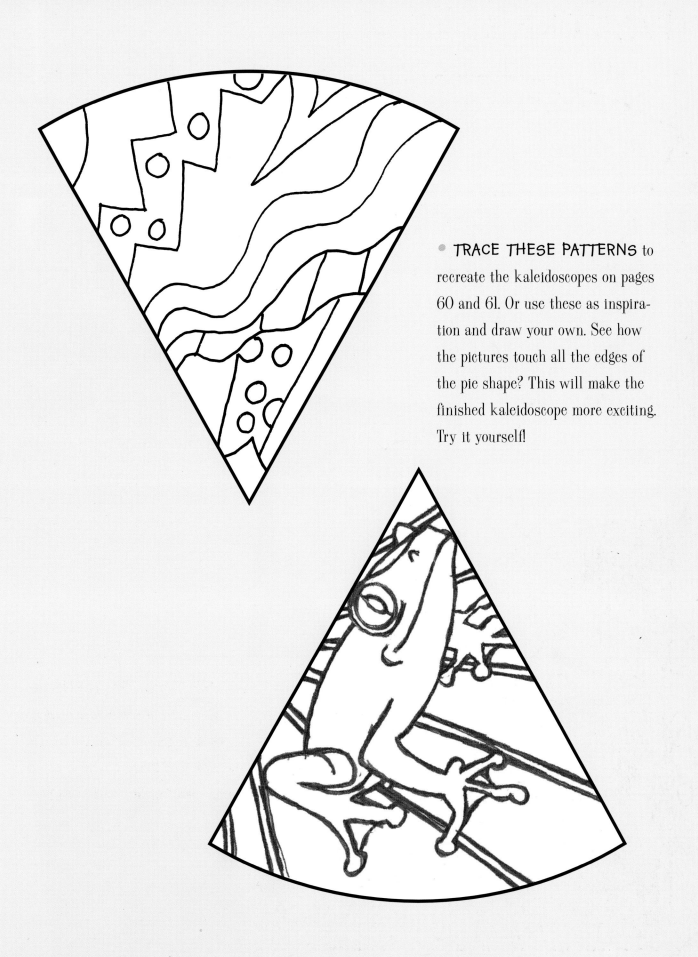

● TRACE THESE PATTERNS to recreate the kaleidoscopes on pages 60 and 61. Or use these as inspiration and draw your own. See how the pictures touch all the edges of the pie shape? This will make the finished kaleidoscope more exciting. Try it yourself!

More fun books for CREATIVE KIDS!

You can make incredible crafts using materials found just outside your window! Learn how to create pressed flower bookmarks, clay tiles, leaf prints, pebble mosaics, nature mobiles and souvenir pillows. You can use collected leaves, rocks, feathers and other natural treasures.

ISBN 1-58180-292-7, paperback, 64 pages, #32169-K

Hey kids! You can create amazing creatures, incredible toys and wild gifts for your friends and family. All it takes is some paint, a few rocks and your imagination! Easy-to-follow pictures and instructions show you how to turn stones into something cool-racecars, bugs, lizards, teddy bears and more.

ISBN 1-58180-255-2, paperback, 64 pages, #32085-K

Oh, the things you can create with paper! Learn how to make paper stars, party streamers, lanterns, hanging baskets, paper beads, handmade books, decoupage and more. These crafts are perfect for parties, rainy days and gift giving, plus they're easy to do and fun to make.

ISBN 1-58180-290-0, paperback, 64 pages, #32167-K

These and other fun North Light books are available from your local art & craft retailer, bookstore, online supplier or by calling **1-800-448-0915.**

Take a batch of colorful polymer clay and transform it into a fantasy world right out of your imagination. Sculptor Maureen Carlson provides basic techniques for sculpting dozens of different creatures, including dragons, lizards, goblins, fairies, pigs, dogs, horses, snakes and more!

ISBN 1-58180-286-2, paperback, 64 pages, #32161-K